Action Sports

Judo

Bill Gutman

Illustrated with photographs by Peter Ford

Editorial Consultant: Tom Crone, Fifth-Degree Black Belt

Capstone Press

MINNEAPOLIS

Printed in the United States of America.

Capstone Press • 2440 Fernbrook Lane • Minneapolis, MN 55447

Editorial Director   John Coughlan
Managing Editor   John Martin
Production Editor   James Stapleton
Copy Editor   Thomas Streissguth

Library of Congress Cataloging-in-Publication Data

Gutman, Bill.
   Judo / Bill Gutman.
     p. cm.
   Includes bibliographical references and index.
   Summary: Describes the Japanese art and sport of judo including a brief history, preparation for training, and techniques of the various throws. Includes a glossary of terms.
   ISBN 1-56065-265-9
   1. Judo--Juvenile literature. [1. Judo.] I. Title
GV1114.G88 1996
796.8'152--dc20   95-7104
                            CIP
                            AC

99 98 97 96 95   6 5 4 3 2 1

Table of Contents

Chapter 1 What is Judo? 5

Chapter 2 Starting Out 9

Chapter 3 Breakfalls... 15

Chapter 4 Getting Ready to Throw 23

Chapter 5 Throws and Counter Throws 29

Chapter 6 Grappling... 39

Glossary 44

To Learn More 46

Some Useful Addresses 47

Index 48

Chapter 1

What is Judo?

Judo is a sport and a form of exercise that came from ju-jitsu, a Japanese martial art. Jigoro Kano, a young Japanese man who had studied ju-jitsu, created judo. A weak and sickly child, Kano took up ju-jitsu to become stronger.

Ju-jitsu did wonders for Kano, but it also held dangers. Kano wanted to create something that anyone could learn and enjoy safely. The result was judo. Kano dropped the striking techniques and more dangerous holds and locks of ju-jitsu. He also wrote rules that insured safety.

The Gentle Way

Judo means "the gentle way." Unlike ju-jitsu, judo uses the idea of giving way to an opponent. Judo fighters use the opponent's force and power against the opponent. That's how a skilled judoist can throw a larger and stronger opponent through the air and onto the ground.

Professor Kano created judo in 1882. By the early 20th century, judo had found its way to many other countries. Japanese immigrants brought judo to the United States and Canada. Today, millions enjoy judo worldwide.

Learning to fall is the first thing a judo student will study. Throwing and grappling come later.

Chapter 2

Starting Out

You can't learn judo on your own. If you want to learn judo, you must find a **dojo,** a place where judo is taught. You also need partners to practice with and a qualified **sensei,** or judo instructor. The sensei keeps order in the dojo and teaches the skills.

In a good dojo, students and teachers show each other respect. They do not practice the skills in a mean or angry way. A dojo should be

The judo outfit–white cotton jacket, pants, and belt–is called a judogi. The color of the belt shows the skill level of the student.

a friendly and helpful place, and learning judo should be fun.

The Judogi

Gi means outfit. The outfit you wear to do judo is a **judogi.** It is made of strong white cotton that can survive judo's powerful grabs and pulls. It should be loose, comfortable, and very clean. It has no buttons or fastenings. A

The shoulder throw is one of the basic judo moves.

The judo thrower always keeps a good grip on the opponent during a throw.

cotton belt around the waist, knotted at the front, holds the judogi in place.

Belt colors show the skill level of the judoist. The black-belt rank, or dan grade, means "expert." There are ten degrees of black belt, but only a few judoists have earned a tenth-degree black belt since the sport began. Ninth degrees are very uncommon, and no non-

Japanese has ever achieved that level. To become a black belt in judo is harder than in most martial arts. Earning higher degress of black belt in judo is also more difficult.

All ranks below black belt are called kyu, meaning "beginner" or "novice." There are usually six kyu grades below black belt. But different judo associations have different ranks and belt colors.

Before You Begin

Judo is an excellent way to get into shape. But to avoid injuries, beginners should only try what their bodies can handle. That way, their progress will come more quickly. A good sensei will make sure that you warm up before beginning practice. As in all sports, warming up, stretching, and doing strength-building exercises are all important in judo.

In a sacrifice throw, such as this circle throw, the judoist gives up a standing position to get the advantage.

Chapter 3
Breakfalls

Judoists throw their partners or opponents so that they land strongly and fully upon their backs. In practice, students take many falls. It seems amazing that they can do this over and over, get up smiling, and do more falls. It is all a matter of using the proper technique in the ukemi, or **breakfall**. Done right, being thrown by a judo partner is completely painless and harmless.

Judoists use a mat, but good ukemi is still necessary. Never try judo without a shock-absorbing surface. And don't try it without the proper instruction and supervision.

Basic Breakfalls

Human beings don't fall well. To do a good breakfall, the student must forget some habits. There are also some basic rules: Never stick out your hand to stop your fall. Never hold your breath. Always keep your chin tucked toward your chest, so the back of your head won't slam down on the mat.

There are three kinds of falls. Sidefalls are the most common. In a backfall, the judoist falls directly on the middle of the back. Rolling falls can be done either forward or backward, and either staying down or getting up with the roll.

To prevent a shock to the chest or to the body's vital organs, the judoist slaps the mat with the cupped palm of the hand and the underside of the forearm at an angle out from the body. The leg does the same, absorbing the rest of the shock. An entire class practicing falling can sound like thunder.

A student prepares for a practice fall.

The Side Backfall

This is the most common way to fall in judo. To practice it, the student lies on the ground and brings the arm up and across the chest to the far ear. While keeping the head off the mat, the student slaps the mat with both arm and leg, first one side, then the other, rolling from side to side. The elbow, and the outside of the knee or ankle, should never hit the mat.

Once this becomes automatic, the student can try falling from a squatting position. Then he can try the sidefall from a standing position. He bends the supporting leg and lowers the body before dropping to the mat.

The sensei decides when the student is ready to take a real fall. During a throw, the thrower holds onto one sleeve while flexing the knees. This eases the impact of the fall.

The Rear Backfall and Rolling Backfall

The rear backfall is just like the sidefall, except that both hands hit at the same time, and

Extending the arm from the body and slapping the mat with the open palm are important during a fall.

the legs go up into the air. In the rolling backfall, the legs keep going up and over completely. It is almost like a rear somersault, except that the head is tucked out of the way and never touches the mat. The student rolls over and comes up to a balanced, standing position.

Rolling Front Falls

This fall also looks like a somersault, but it is done over one arm, which acts like a wheel. The student rolls over that arm and across the back, rather than over the top of the head. The student may stay down and slap for this move. Or, he may keep going through the roll and come to a balanced, standing position.

None of the rolling falls should be tried without proper instruction and supervision. For safety, falls and throws should always be done slowly at the beginning.

In the rolling backfall, the student rolls backwards over the shoulder, almost like in a rear somersault. But the head should not touch the mat.

Chapter 4

Getting Ready to Throw

Throwing requires special skills. A throw is much more than just picking someone up and throwing them down. The judoist uses the other person's motion against them. But when most people first learn to throw, the partner stands still. This helps the student get all the moves right.

Judo Postures

There are two important judo postures: **natural posture** and **defensive posture**. Both provide excellent balance, whether the judoist is standing still or moving. Students try to get the opponent to move into an unbalanced motion or position. This makes a throw possible.

In natural posture, the judoist stands with feet shoulder-width apart. His weight is centered over the hips, with the knees slightly bent. He begins moving from the abdomen and hips, instead of from the upper body. In natural posture, the feet stay even or one foot moves forward of the other, either to the right or left.

The defensive posture is used while blocking an attack. The legs spread farther apart, and the knees bend more deeply.

The judoist moves mostly in the natural posture. He looks for a chance to upset the opponent's balance.

Getting a Grip

In judo, both players hold onto the judogi of the other. There are many different grips, but beginners always use a standard grip. One hand holds the opponent's sleeve just behind and

Judoists in defensive posture use the standard grip. One arm grips the opponent's sleeve. The other grips the opposite lapel.

under the elbow. The other holds the lapel at chest level, usually just below the collarbone.

The arms should be slightly bent and relaxed. Their weight pulls downward slightly on the opponent. The last three fingers make

The Major Outer Reap.

the main grab, while the index finger and thumb hardly close at all. The grip is firm but not rigid. The better judoists become, the more lightly they grip.

Most beginners will grab too strongly and stiffen their arms out straight. This feels natural, but it is not a good defense. Looseness, flexibility, quickness, and mobility are the best defense.

Moving and Breaking Balance

Movement is everything in judo. The idea is to keep your balance while breaking the balance of the other person. If pushed, yield and pull. If pulled, yield and push.

There are eight directions of off-balancing: front, back, left side, right side, and the four corners. All judo throws push the opponent off-balance in one of those directions.

Every step creates an opportunity. Every move gives the judoist a split second to unbalance and throw the opponent.

Chapter 5

Throws and Counter Throws

At first, judo experts created 40 basic throws. Most were offensive moves. But judo, like any modern sport, is always changing. Today, there are 65 basic throws. Many of the extra 25 are counter throws.

All throws fall into five basic groups: hand throws, hip throws, leg and foot throws, and two kinds of sacrifice throws–side and back. And every throw has three parts: unbalancing, fitting the body in place, and completing the throw.

The Body Drop

The Body Drop

As the opponent steps forward with the right foot, the thrower pulls with the left hand. This moves the opponent off balance to the right front corner. Turning in the same direction, the thrower moves both hands in a circular motion. He steps across with the right leg, places it below the knee for leverage, and throws the opponent.

The One-Arm Shoulder Throw

The thrower brings the opponent off balance to the front. The thrower releases the lapel hand grip. While turning around and under the opponent's center of balance, he pulls the opponent and traps his arm. From this position, the thrower bends forward in a curling motion. He springs up with the legs and turns to the right. This carries the opponent up and over his shoulder and onto the mat.

These are two very popular tournament throws. They are examples of the many hand techniques in judo.

The Major Hip Throw

This is one of the very first throws beginners learn. It looks simple, but many judoists have won world titles with it.

The thrower breaks his opponent's balance to the front. The thrower then pulls with the right hand and steps in with the right foot. The right hand releases the collar grip, and the left foot moves in. The thrower pushes his hip across the front of the opponent's body below the center of balance. The right arm holds the opponent's body to the rear hip.

Both of the thrower's feet should be inside the opponent's feet, and the arm around the waist should not be at a backward angle to the thrower. The thrower twists with his upper body. The arm pulls and the legs spring to throw the opponent across the hips and to the mat.

The Sweeping Hip Throw

This throw is similar to the major hip throw, except the hip doesn't go in and across as deeply, and the unbalancing is more to the right

In the sweeping hip throw, the thrower sweeps back and up with the right leg to throw the opponent.

front corner. The hand does not have to go behind the back. Usually, it continues to hold the collar or grips the back of the opponent's neck.

The thrower brings the opponent forward on the opponent's right foot. The thrower steps in

and makes body contact. He then uses his right leg to sweep upward and backward against the opponent's right leg.

The Sliding Foot Sweep

In judo, sliding the feet together can be a big mistake. The thrower can use the foot on the same side as the opponent's trailing foot to sweep the opponent's feet together. The hand on the same side as the sweeping foot goes down and under. The other hand goes up and over. The result is a spectacular airborne flight.

The major outer reap is almost the opposite of the sweeping hip throw. As the opponent steps forward with the right foot, the thrower steps forward with the left foot. She places it behind the opponent's rear right corner point of balance.

The thrower pulls down and inward with the sleeve holding hand, and pulls the opponent closer with the lapel hand. The thrower can now use the right leg in a large, circular, sweeping motion. She carries the opponent up and over with the leg.

Sacrifice Throws

"Sacrifice" means giving up your standing position to unbalance the opponent. These throws are done by falling to the back or to the side.

Back Sacrifice–The Circle Throw

The thrower falls to the ground in a rounded back position. He brings the opponent forward and downward. As the opponent starts to tip forward, the thrower brings his foot up into the opponent's waist. This carries the opponent up and over in a large circle. The ability to do the two-handed backfall comes in handy for the circle throw.

As the opponent steps forward, the thrower falls in front at an angle. He extends the left leg and pulls the opponent over in a circle. The leg doesn't actually trip the opponent. Instead, it allows the thrower to use both feet and the back of the left shoulder to add power to the throw. A good front roll fall will help the person being thrown.

Counter Throws

Sometimes a judo thrower does not do a good job of unbalancing his opponent. The opponent can then try a counter throw.

The Reverse Hip Throw

One judoist steps in to try a front hip throw. But the other player bends the knees into a defensive posture. He pulls the first knee inward. With an upward thrust of the hips, he can push his opponent into the air and back down onto the mat.

As the first player steps in for a throw, the other drops into a position behind. The extended leg catches the opponent's legs behind the knees. The thrower turns toward the other player so that they land almost chest-to-chest.

Chapter 6

Grappling

There is more to judo than throwing. When a throw does not land the opponent on his back, players often continue the action on the mat. Grappling techniques include hold-downs, **chokes**, and arm locks. The goal is to get the opponent to submit.

Hold-Downs

Judoists often use hold-downs to win a victory. For a win, the judoist must keep control of the opponent for thirty seconds.

The Valley Drop is a counter throw. The girl on the right prepares to drop her opponent.

Of course, no opponent will simply lie down and lose. Both players are always careful not to get into a choke or armbar. For every hold-down, there are ways to escape. But once you're caught in one, getting out is very hard.

The scarf hold is one of the most common hold-downs. It is easy to get to from a throw. After the throw, the sleeve arm is controlled. The player sits so the hip goes into the opponent's arm pit. He holds the sleeve arm strongly across the chest and under the left arm. The right arm cradles the neck, keeping the opponent from pushing against the mat with his head.

In the upper four-corner hold, the opponent is held down by pressure on the chest and upper body. The person on top passes both arms under the opponent's arms and grabs the belt, then uses the legs, either spread out to avoid being turned over, or up close to the opponent's shoulders to lessen the opponent's upper body strength.

After the throw, judoists maneuver for good position on the mat.

In the vertical four-corner hold, one player is directly on top of the other, pressing from belly to chest. The opponent's arm is trapped against the side of the head by both arms and the side of the neck. The holder uses outward pressure to trap the opponent's legs.

Choke Holds

These holds apply pressure on the side of the neck. They are not done against the

In the side four-corner hold, the opponent is unable to use his legs or arms. The match will soon be over.

windpipe–that could cause serious injury. Chokes are meant to force a surrender, not to injure. Judoists under thirteen are not allowed to use them.

When he wants to surrender, the opponent will slap the mat or tap on the other player. If the hands are trapped, the foot is used to tap out. When this signal is given, the judoist should stop any action immediately.

Armbars are also meant to force surrender. In practice, and even in competition, it is important to apply these very carefully. When players resist, the arm can give way very quickly. The person applying the hold must be careful not to let the arm overextend. In most competitions, people under the age of sixteen are not allowed to use armbars.

An armhold can quickly force a surrender.

Glossary

belt color—the symbol for the skill level of a person practicing judo. In most schools, as their skills increase, students wear differently colored belts. Black belts always represent the highest skill levels.

breakfall—the technique judoists use to soften the impact of a fall. Slapping the mat with the hand and arm at the moment of impact is the major part of the breakfall.

breaking balance—moving an opponent off his or her **center of gravity**. Breaking an opponent's balance is the first step in preparing to make a throw.

center of gravity—the body's balancing point. In judo, the hips should be centered right above the feet. Keeping a correct center of gravity makes it harder for someone to move you.

choke—a hold that applies pressure to the carotid artery of the neck. This can be dangerous if the person applying the choke does not release as soon as his opponent taps him.

defensive posture—the position someone takes when he or she is getting ready to block an opponent's offensive move. The knees are bent, and the weight is lowered.

dojo—the place where people practice and teach judo

hold-down—a technique to keep an opponent down on the mat

judogi—the cotton suit worn while practicing judo

natural posture—a starting position with feet shoulder-width apart, knees bent slightly. The natural posture provides a solid center of gravity from which to attack or defend.

sensei—a judo instructor

To Learn More

Barrett, Norman. *Martial Arts.* New York: Franklin Watts, 1988.

Casey, Kevin. *Judo.* Vero Beach, Florida: Rourke, 1994.

Dando, Justin. *Judo.* New York: Sterling, 1990.

Ribner, Susan and Richard Chin. *The Martial Arts.* New York: Harper & Row, 1978.

Magazines:

Black Belt
24715 Avenue Rockefeller
Santa Clarita, CA 91380

Some Useful Addresses

Kodokan
1-16-30, Kasuga
Bunkyo-ku, Tokyo
Japan

United States Judo Federation
19 N. Union Boulevard
Colorado Springs, CO 80909

United States Judo, Inc.
P.O. Box 10013
El Paso, TX 79991

Judo Canada
333 River Road
Ottawa, Ontario K11 8H9
Canada

Index

armbars, 39-40, 42-43

belts, 10-11, 13, 44
black belts, 11, 13
breakfalls, 15-21, 37, 44
    rear backfall, 18, 21; rolling
    backfall, 21; rolling front
    falls, 21; side backfalls, 16,
    18

Canada, 7

dojo, 9

exercises, 13

grips, 24-25, 27, 31-32

injuries, 13, 15
instructors, 9, 12, 18

Japan, 7
ju-jitsu, 5, 7
judogi, 10, 24

Kano, Jigoro, 5, 7

mats, 15, 21, 37

off-balancing, 27, 31

postures, 23-24, 37, 44

rules, 5

safety, 5, 21
slapping, 16, 18, 21, 42, 44
stretching, 13

throws, 29, 31-33, 35-37, 39-
    40
    body drop, 31; circle throw,
    36; major hip throw, 32;
    one-arm shoulder throw,
    31; reverse hip throw, 37;
    sliding foot sweep, 35-36;
    sweeping hip throw, 33, 35

United States, 7